Still Born

It's Going To Happen

Glenda Woods

My Scribe Publishing

Contents

Still Born	v
Acknowledgments	ix
Preface	xiii
Introduction	xxi
1. The Revelation of the "Still Born" Baby	1
2. Beside the Still Waters	5
3. Still . . . In Agreement	11
4. Resuscitation	26
5. Take Up Thy Bed And Walk	33
6. Weight . . . On the Lord	44
7. Worth the Wait	52
My Daily Prayer	57
References	59
Numbers 23:19	61

Still Born

Glenda Woods

Still Born

By Glenda Woods

Copyright © 2023 by Glenda Woods

All rights reserved. No part of this publication may be reproduced, distributed, or transmitted in any form or by any means, including, photocopying, recording, or other electronic or mechanical methods, without the prior written permission, except in the case of brief quotations embodied in critical reviews and certain other noncommercial uses permitted by copyright law.

ISBN: 978-1-7379354-5-2

Printed in the United States of America

Published by My Scribe Publishing

IN LOVING MEMORY OF

Pastor James W. Brock, Sr.
&
Pastor Mary Mitchell

Acknowledgments

First, I would like to acknowledge my Heavenly Father whom I love so passionately. I honor you for who You are, for all You have done, for all you are doing right now, and for all You are going to do. Without You, none of this would be possible. It's ALL about YOU.

To my wonderful husband and pastor, Leroy Woods III (United Rock of Ages M. B. Church), I can't thank God enough for bringing us together. I truly enjoy serving with you in ministry. You are an honorable man and an awesome pastor. I genuinely appreciate all of your love, support, prayers, and protection as God continues to send us forth.

To my beautifully unique children [Pierre (Shaikenya), Mary, and Leroy IV], thank all of you for taking this journey with me. You have yet to see all that God is going to do in your lives if you remain faithful to Him, and always remember our signature scripture (Psalms 37:25).

To my wonderful grand angels (Erin, Olivia, and Audrey), your love and smiles keep me motivated.

To my biological and first spiritual mother, Mary Brock, I can't thank you enough for your continued guidance, prayers, love, and support. Thank you for teaching me the correlation between natural and spiritual. If it had not been for your sacrifices, I would not have developed into this vessel that I have become.

To my sisters and brother [Debra (Gene); Arletha (Pete); Arvelia; Junice; and James, Jr.], thanks for supporting me in all that I do. Always remember to govern your lives by Matthew 6:33.

To Dr. Henry and Doretha Knox (St. Peter M. B. Church), thank you for all of the love and guidance I received while serving in your ministry and for our life-long friendship. To my spiritual covering, Bishop Roderick and Lady Helen Mitchell [New Life Church], thanks for all of your love, prayers, development, and support.

To my aunts, uncles, nieces, nephews, cousins, extended family, in-laws, colleagues, former teachers, former students, and many friends, I love and appreciate all of you. You have always been encouraging and supportive.

To United Rock of Ages M. B. Church, MCC, The Filling Station Family, Our House, and all of my faith-filled prayer partners, I truly appreciate your continued love, prayers, and support.

Preface

In mid-January 2020, I found myself in one of the most indecisive stages of my life. I had come into the new year with renewed faith and great aspirations for this leap year or year of redemption, but I knew that internally something was different. Yes, I had just released a new music project in the latter part of 2019, but there was no real excitement or inner peace. Fear had set in, and I began questioning some of the decisions I had made. It always seemed like no matter how hard I worked or how committed I was that things were not working consistently in my favor. Seemingly, we would have a good start and then things would shut down. I was in the marketing stages of the new music project, but things weren't coming together. I was doing a lot, but I wasn't accomplishing much. Although I encountered some successes near the end of 2019, things were not really connecting as I had desired. Things were moving really slow. This is when the struggle really began. Actually, I had become overwhelmed.

A couple of months passed, and we were getting ready for Spring Break. I had found some renewed motivation. I had planned a radio promotions road trip from Jackson, MS to the Gulf Coast. Everything was in motion until I started getting a few cancellations. Little did I know that we were about to embark upon a pandemic (unlike anything we had ever experienced before). We received notices from our employers that we would not be returning to the building until further notice. At that point, the media began releasing more and more information about COVID-19 and the possibility of there being a complete shutdown of everything. Panic set in.

There was indeed a shutdown, and life, as we had known it, changed completely. Travel was shut down; engagements/events were canceled; people were in a state of fear and uncertainty because of the virus. The success of everything I had been preparing for was predicated upon my being able to get out and promote the project as well as continue in the church ministry work that I was already doing.

So there I was near the end of March wondering how I would recoup the money I had spent, how I would maintain mobility, or just where I would go from here. Every time I attempted to do some things via social media, roadblocks surfaced, and I eventually lost my momentum. I just wasn't feeling it. Also, I was at a place where I didn't want to be doing random stuff just to stay visible. I wanted God's blessing to be on whatever I did. Time continued to pass, and we were still in partial quarantine in an effort to combat or slow the spread of the virus.

By mid-April, things began to intensify. I found myself becoming more and more discouraged. We were still ministering to others, helping them get through what they were going through, but I was not properly addressing what I was going through. It had gotten to a point where I had to come face-to-face with my own personal battles—my own personal struggles. Through much personal prayer and intercession, God began to clarify what was going on with me, and the journey began to unfold.

I literally had to ask myself, "Where do I go from here?" I felt that I had nothing else to give—but giving up was not an option. This was one time that I did not have an answer. In addition, my drive... my tenacity ... and my energy were deeply buried beneath all of the hurt, the disappointments, and the fear. So, I began spending more and more time daily in prayer, seeking God's guidance and direction for my life. Each day during my daily walk, I would talk to the Lord, and I would listen to what He had to say. I went from pleading, begging, and crying to receiving and believing. Although we started our journey on January 23, 2020, He did not begin to release this word until October 18, 2020—nine months later.

> At 9:00 AM, October 18th, He led me to Psalms 23:2 which states, *"He maketh me to lie down in green pastures: he leadeth me beside the still waters."*

As I was reading, the Lord had me to pin "still waters." He had me to carefully look at the word "still" which means motionless, stationary, at rest, quiet, silent, calm, and tranquil. He was leading me to this shallow yet peaceful place —a place of tranquility to rest from my busy schedule long enough to hear Him. This was our opportunity to spend intimate time together so that He could refresh me and give me direction for the journey ahead.

So, here I am at this place in my life with a calling and many assignments to complete, but at a much older age. For so many years (36+) I had been holding on to the promise and serving faithfully, but at this point/stage, I had begun to feel that it was too late. In our time together, God took me back to Abraham and Sarah in *Genesis 21*. He reminded me that just as He fulfilled the promise to Abraham of being the Father of Many Nations and to Sarah by giving birth to a son, He would fulfill His promise to me. This stood out because Abraham (100) and Sarah (90) were well-past child-bearing age when Isaac was born. Not only that, but God made the promise to Abraham at age 75 in *Genesis 12*. This was an example that just because things take a long time to manifest, it doesn't mean that they won't happen. We just have to trust the process.

God wanted to remind me that Isaac was ***still born***, but it happened when his parents were probably at a place where they had stopped fully believing and in a position where they no longer had control over the end results. The significant thing about this is that God promised Abraham that he would be the Father of Many Nations, but it would not happen until he and Sarah gave birth to a child. He did it for them, and He assured me that everything He promised was **still** going to happen *(Num. 23:19)*. He is **still** going to finish what He started in me *(Phil. 1:6)*.

Introduction

I wallowed in my fears and shed many tears for years and years. I looked the part and pretended that all was well when it was really not. It was so painful knowing that God had called me to something greater, but there was so much uncertainty as to how or when it would manifest. I knew the word said that I would "reap" in "due season" if I could just hang in there, but the wait started to weigh heavily upon me. I kept pressing my way and trying at all costs to fulfill the calling upon my life. Eventually, I began to feel that no matter how faithful I had been that I wasn't good enough, that I wasn't as qualified as some others were, or even financially stable enough. I had so much bottled up on the inside that I began to lose focus.

I knew what God had spoken and I continued to pursue it wholeheartedly, but the investments I had made didn't seem to be paying off. It even looked like the unfaithful and the uncommitted were going forth, but I wasn't. I couldn't understand what was going on, so I came to a place in my life where I began to believe that it was just not going to happen... and in 2020, I gave up. I didn't know what to do, and for the first time in my life, I had no answers. I didn't even have the energy to fake it anymore, but God sent some special faith-filled midwives along the way to force me to push. They saw what I could no longer see. From that push, things began to unfold, and God is allowing me to confidently step into my destiny.

There are so many of you who are at the same crossroad right now. You have been going through the motions. You have been asking yourself, "What's the purpose of staying faithful and committed?" You have stopped praying. You have stopped believing wholeheartedly. You are thinking about giving up on what God has spoken, but God says, "No! You can't give up."

You are the reason He has given me the assignment to write <u>Still Born</u>. Therefore, those of you who have a dream, a vision, a calling... and even to those who have been operating in what you believe you were called to do but you have been struggling, "THINGS ARE ABOUT TO TURN AROUND IN YOUR LIFE." God is allowing me to see what you no longer see, and what He sees for us is greater than what we initially saw. (*Eph. 3:20*) As you travel with me through my experiences in <u>Still Born</u>, I pray that you will allow the Holy Spirit to speak to your heart in reference to your own journey because if God spoke it and you follow His steps, He is going to make it good. (*Num. 23:19*)

IT'S GOING TO HAPPEN

Chapter 1

The Revelation of the "Still Born" Baby

Natural vs. Spiritual

At 8:48 PM, April 28, 2020, my thoughts were all over the place. I was still struggling with whether I should give up on the things I had been assigned or whether to stay in the fight. Just as the battle began to intensify, God began to drop some things in my spirit. As He began to speak, I began to write. He began to show me the correlation between a stillborn baby in the natural versus a stillborn baby in the spirit. According to *Wikipedia*, "Stillbirth is typically defined as fetal death at or after 20 to 28 weeks of pregnancy." The baby is born **without signs of life**. Therefore, it is dead upon delivery/arrival. One thing I found quite interesting is that although the fetus has all major body organs at this stage, they will not be fully developed and functional. Also, some organs are not even in their proper location during this stage. In comparison/contrast, He showed me that when the spiritual gift (baby) is conceived (formed/devised), it is born **with signs of life**, packaged with everything it needs; however, it will not be fully developed and functional and some things will not be in their proper place at that time.

I was thinking, "I can kind of see this, but how does it all really relate?" "What does it mean to be STILL BORN?" The word "*still*" kept resonating in my spirit so I began to research it. **Still** is an interesting word that has four different meanings which function as four different parts of speech. However, we are looking at **_still_** as an adjective and as an adverb. As an adjective, it means not moving or making a sound (motionless, immobile, at rest, lifeless). As an adverb, it means up to and including the present or the time mentioned (referring to something that will or may happen in the future). In this particular analogy, we are examining **still** as an adjective in the natural (Stillborn) and **still** as an adverb in the spiritual (Still Born).

As I began to dig deeper into the study of **still**, I noticed that in the natural stillborn is a compound word, a derivative of the noun stillbirth. The words still and birth/born are used together to form a new meaning. It is categorized as a closed compound word which initially was written as two separate words. Nevertheless, as two separate words, **still** functions as an adjective which describes or modifies birth/born. In this case, it meant motionless, lifeless, dead, or deceased.

From the spiritual perspective of this text, **still** functions as an adverb which modifies the verb **born**. Structurally speaking, still born is a verb phrase. One thing I noticed in the definition of the word ***adverb*** is that it *modifies* or *qualifies* the verb. According to *Dictionary.com*, to modify anything means to "make partial or minor changes to (something), typically so as to improve it or to make it less extreme." To qualify means "to become officially recognized by fulfilling or satisfying the relevant conditions or requirements (fit, equipped, prepared, seasoned)." Yes, the baby has been conceived, but God has the power and authority to modify and qualify prior to the full manifestation. It's in His hands.

Chapter 2

Beside the Still Waters

***Psalms 23:1-2* (KJV)** "The LORD [is] my shepherd; I shall not want. He maketh me to lie down in green pastures: he leadeth me beside the still waters."

Still – quiet; hushed; noiseless; silent; calm; free from turbulence

Here we are again on October 18, 2020, around 9:00 PM and the Lord takes me to **Psalm 23:2** which states, *"He maketh me to lie down in green pastures: he leadeth me beside the still* *waters.*" I took a few notes and let this rest for two years.

As I began revisiting **Psalm 23:2** on August 10, 2022, and the meaning of still, I could remember so clearly in my childhood when my mom would press or straighten our hair. When she would get extremely close to what we called "the kitchen" or back scalp, we would start twitching and moving. THAT COMB WAS HOT!!! She would shout repeatedly, "Be still!" In other words, if we were constantly moving, we could get burned. We needed to be real still because the hot comb had to get as close to the scalp as possible to straighten out the nappy hair. She wanted the roots to be smooth just like the rest of the hair. Interestingly, she and my dad would do the same thing if they were whipping us. They would whip and shout, "Be still!" It was painful, but they wanted us to sit still and take it because the more we moved, the longer it took for them to get finished.

God enlightened me at this point, He said that we are not listening to Him when we are constantly moving and twitching and always in a hurry. In other words, just like with our natural parents, we might as well sit still and take it. We are going to get the lecture, the instructions, or the whipping anyway on their terms, so we may as well stop prolonging the process.

In both analogies, there was a significant correlation between heat and still. Spiritually speaking, it can get really heated in those moments of discipline, and it's imperative that we are still long enough to get straightened out. He needs time to make the crooked places "straight" and the rough ways "smooth." (*Luke 3:5b*) As I am writing now, I can hear Him saying, "These 'still moments' are a part of the process. It paces you and keeps you on track." I can also hear, "Be still, and know that I am God." [*Psalm 46:10 KJV*] The *NET* version says, "... Stop your striving and know that I am God."

God took me back to *Psalms 23:2*. He had me to look at the verse even more closely. Part *A* states, "He maketh me to lie down in green pastures," which means he makes, compels, or constrains me. It's not a choice. He requires me to "lie down" or rest. Sometimes He has to arrest or take us into custody in order to get our attention. He halts things so that we can check or take a good look at the progress of the process. He's not afraid to apprehend us and interrupt, put an end to, or slow some things down in order to get us back on track.

Now that I'm resting, I am still enough to hear what He wants to say. He then has me to focus on *Part B* of verse **2**. It is only after He makes me rest or restrains me that He leads or guides me beside the still (peaceful/comfortable) waters. His order is to rest...before taking the next step. One thing He opened my eyes to was that if I was unwilling to settle down or receive the "rest," then I would be unable to follow His leading. He then leads me to a place where there are no distractions. I can focus on Him. I can be refreshed.

Another thing that He emphasized was the word "beside" He leads us "beside" (alongside or next to) and not "in" the still waters. Sometimes we can be so restless on this journey that God takes us by the side of something so we can get a clearer picture of what it looks like. In this instance, we can see what peace, stillness, or rest really looks like. "Beside" gives us an opportunity to see what "still waters" look like. The reflection from the waters can also help us see what we look like. As water is symbolic of the word, it gives us a mirrored image. It gives us a better perspective of what He's trying to show us.

As I continued to meditate and think about "rest," I was taken back to the cooking shows that I like to watch on television. They are always talking about the temperature of the meat when it's done and how to let it set after cooking.

I remembered emphasis being put on why all meat should rest after cooking. When meat is cooked, the proteins in the meat heat up and set. At this point, all of the juices are pushed toward the center of the meat. The meat then has to be pulled away from the heat to stand or rest before serving so that the juices can be redistributed throughout the meat. It is always suggested that meat should rest at least half the time it is cooked which makes it tender and juicy, and much easier to consume.

From a spiritual perspective, if something has been cooking in us or developing in us, we need to give it time to rest before putting it out there. The scripture teaches in *2 Timothy 2:20-21* that God wants us to be useful, profitable, and prepared for the work. When we "rest" and everything is redistributed or settled, we are then ready to be used by God for His glory.

Chapter 3

Still... In Agreement

Proverbs 3:5 (KJV) "Trust in the Lord with all thine heart; and lean not unto thine own understanding."

Trust – confidence; belief; faith

Agreement – harmony; consistency; understanding

On December 29, 2020 at 9:11 PM, God began to speak to me in reference to what "Still in Agreement" means. He said, "It means Under My Terms. Read the Contract." Then He said, "Especially the *fine*

***print*.**" "You've been spending too much time looking at what I said I would do, but not enough time focusing on the specifics." The fine print is representative of the word of God which is there to clarify the terms of the contract or the path or direction to follow. In other words, it should be "a lamp unto our feet and a light unto our paths." (*Psalm 119:105*) He said, "If you don't know what we are supposed to be in agreement about there are going to be some disputes, and before I can allow you to move forward in representing my corporation, we've got to be on the same page." At this point, He began to give me the outline and specifics of this chapter, but I didn't really write a lot down. I jotted down a few notes and then I let it rest until He was ready to move forward.

This chapter rested for approximately a month and a half. During that time, I had been struggling or toiling through some things. I knew what the scripture said, and what God had said about His thoughts and His ways, but it was still a challenge for me to rest easily or to be totally settled in that. My level of contentment was not where it needed to be. I began writing again on February 10, 2021. As I was praying that morning, the Lord impressed upon my spirit that my labor was not in vain in Him. He knew I needed to hear that. Sometimes many stages of the process appear to be in conflict with the end result.

When things didn't turn out as expected, I would often find myself wrestling with the thought that maybe God didn't want me to do those things or maybe I should give that up completely. But the challenge I've always had at this point is that I was assured that He had given me the work or assignment based on how He speaks and operates in our relationship. I would find myself thinking, "Why is this taking so long?" Sometimes I would even do things to try and speed the process up, but it just didn't work. As I was listening to Him, *1 Cor. 15:58* illuminated in my spirit. It states, "Therefore, my beloved brethren, be ye steadfast, unmoveable, always abounding in the work of the Lord, forasmuch as ye know that your labour is not in vain in the Lord." He then asked me a couple of questions:

In My Work....

1. Haven't you always been steadfast (unwavering, faithful, loyal, committed)?
2. Haven't you always been unmovable (established, hooked, locked in)?
3. Haven't you always been abounding (plentiful, abundant, overflowing)?

And I'm thinking, "Yes. Yes. Yes." He then said, "Well, you can be confident that your labor has not been in vain."

STOP DOUBTING!!!

STOP STRUGGLING!!!

It's right there in the scripture.

"I gave the assignment(s). Just follow My lead. Your Labor Is Not in Vain."

I knew that, but like so many others after years and years of pushing, pressing, and striving, I began to waver because I didn't see the full manifestation or I began to look at or compare my progress to others. It's easy to get tripped up trying to implement our assignments through the footsteps or paths of others. I often remind myself that we are all different people with different callings or assignments. We have to stay focused on our specific assignment(s). The scripture teaches in Galatians 6:9, *"Let us not be weary in well doing: for in due season we shall reap, if we faint not."* We must keep our focus on God; trust Him; acknowledge Him; and allow Him to direct our paths.

On April 23, 2022, a year later, God began to speak again in reference to

Agreement. Actually, I was standing in my bathroom on that Saturday morning, just thinking about the chapter on Trust and Agreement. The Holy Spirit took me back to Proverbs 3:5 (KJV) which states, *"Trust in the LORD with all thine heart; and lean not unto thine own understanding."* He reiterated that failure to read/study the fine print leads us to making our own decisions about what the contract is saying. There are terms and conditions specified in the fine print, just as there are specific terms and conditions in the Word of God. He then began to unload. It had become evident that I had some trust issues.

Many times we say we trust Him, but we really don't because we have a tendency of trying to figure or work things out for ourselves. If we truly trusted Him, we wouldn't become frustrated.

I heard the phrase "Trust Fund." I began to do a little research because I knew God wanted to open the eyes of my heart to some things I had been missing.

Trust funds consist of assets belonging to a trust, held by the trustees for the beneficiaries." (*Investopedia.com*) He was intentionally leading me to "A Trust." A trust is a relationship in which a trustor gives the trustee the right to hold title to property or assets for a beneficiary. Trusts are established to provide legal protection for the trustor's assets, to make sure those assets are distributed according to the wishes of the trustor. (Investopedia.com)

Spiritually speaking, God (our Trustor) gives us the right to manage the property (gift, calling, etc.) for the benefit of others. Many times we (the trustees) get our roles confused. We begin to think that what God has given us to manage (our gift/talent/calling) is for our benefit. We are rewarded for management, but we are not the designated beneficiary. When we disobey or mishandle God's property, He has to put us in check. He has to show us who owns and controls the assets. He helps us keep it legal. He has to show us where our level of Agreement is. When we are born again, we accept salvation by trusting and believing. God becomes our authority and He sets up and oversees our lives—our spiritual assets (benefits, talents, gifts, blessings). He establishes when to release us or when we are ready to be trusted with management. That's something to really think about.

On May 10, 2022, I found myself asking again, "What is God saying about agreement?" As I was writing, God dropped this nugget in my spirit. *"If you don't know what we are supposed to be in agreement with, there are going to be some disputes, and before I can allow you to move forward in representing my corporation, we've got to be on the same page."* He emphasized that I had been leaning to my own understanding. He then took me back to *Proverbs 3:5-6*.

> I heard Him speak, "Lean NOT…To Your Own Understanding."

I had to stop there a minute and let that rest. God took me back to my notes on October 28, 2020. As we reflect back on being still born, He reminded me that my steps have been ordered by Him, but it had taken so long for some things to manifest that my trust level had become compromised, and I had started "leaning" to my own understanding. Since I wasn't acknowledging Him in ALL my plans, I started directing my own paths.

He directs our steps through His word. I heard the Spirit say, "He 'shall' or intends to move predicated upon our CONDUCT." When He is in control, it becomes "ALL ABOUT HIM" and "NOT" ABOUT US!!! Our daily prayer should be Psalm 119:133 which says, "Order my steps in thy word: and let not any iniquity have dominion over me."

Even after all of this insight, I still found myself asking God, "Well, why did you permit me to do the things that were not your divine will for my life?" He said, "I gave you an opportunity to choose.

What you choose shows where your heart is at that time. But even in those choices, I was preparing you for your destiny. It was a GLORY test. Who was getting the glory, you or Me? I had to break your will in order to infuse my will." When I looked back at my notes on October 18, 2022, I noticed that He was maturing me. At the onset, I was writing or operating from a gift/talent perspective— more about what I had heard or seen. But as He has been taking me through the process, I have begun to write from personal experience whereas He gets all the glory. Let's look at **Matt. 5:13-14** (KJV) which clarifies why we do what we do.

> **13** "Ye are the salt of the earth: but if the salt have lost his savour (taste), wherewith shall it be salted? it is thenceforth good for nothing, but to be cast out, and to be trodden under foot of men. **14** Ye are the light of the world. A city that is set on a hill cannot be hid."

Matthew 5:16 (KJV) says, *"Let your light so shine before men, that they may see your good works,* **and glorify your Father which is in heaven**.*"* Let your light shine in such a way that as God works through you, He will be glorified.

So God decided that He wanted me to take a brief walk down memory lane to help me see more clearly why He permitted me to do some things that were a part of His divine will but were not in the divine season of release. I completed my first book in 2010. I contemplated releasing it from 2011-2014. I made serious plans to release the book in March 2015. This is when the contacts began.

Originally, I had created a name for the publishing company which was *Woods' Ink*. I was using the name in my classroom for our publications. I even developed a logo. I then contacted my graphics designer to create a professional logo for my new company in June 2016. In the latter part of June 2016, he completed the graphic design for the book cover as well as e-blasts and other promotional material. The book cover was beautiful, but I couldn't get settled with it. It had a full picture of me and some other details that really brought out the title of the book. But, every time I looked at the cover, all I could see was me. When I talked with my graphic designer about it, he was convinced that it was the right cover. I liked it, but I wasn't feeling it.

I had initially contacted a publishing company in March 2015. I began working with that company in June 2016. I had met all of their requirements including receiving an ISBN # and was ready to get started. I emailed the transcript to the publishing company. A few weeks later, they sent an email indicating that they were still waiting on the transcript. I couldn't figure out what happened. Also, at that time, I was facing some other timing challenges so I just didn't respond. The company eventually refunded my payment. I even purchased an

LLC for Woods' Ink in May 2016 but never used it. I was paying LLC fees each year in hopes of eventually releasing the book...but nothing happened. The company was dissolved in February 2018.

The Project was not ready in 2015, but I was so determined. I had previously re-released the single "I'm Healed" nationally from my 2006 CD Project with a new video in the fall of that same year. I was so certain that it was time to release the book because it had been heavy in my heart for 4 years. I just felt like I wasn't obeying God's will. When my husband and I talked about timing, I had a hard time understanding why God kept giving me all of these things to do but wouldn't allow me to do them. In July 2016 our Church Mantra was "Grow Up Before You Go Up." God really dealt with me. I wanted to release the book before I fully got what God wanted me to get or realize that He was speaking to me. I had to go back and make some apologies.

After the conference, God impressed upon me to revisit the manuscript and begin writing. There was something He wanted to show me. The plot had thickened. I was getting ready to release a book that was not finished. The climax was missing. I was trying to release the book in third person, but He wanted me to release it in first person because it was about me. He also had me to revisit the name and logo of the publishing company (Woods' Ink). It was not what He wanted. I was trying to get the glory for His work and didn't realize it. He then gave me the name and logo He desired based on the work we would be doing in the future from the company that He established. [To God be the glory.]

When we bring this all together, we have to look back at *Isaiah 55:8-9*.

> **8** "For my thoughts [are] not your thoughts, neither [are] your ways my ways, saith the LORD. For [as] the heavens are higher than the earth, so

are my ways higher than your ways, and my thoughts than your thoughts."

As I'm looking at this reference, this is the first time I've paid close attention to verse **9**. The word *"higher"* has become so much clearer. When we lean to our own understanding and don't acknowledge Him, we are limited. We put limitations on what God wants to do. His plan is to do something bigger, something greater, something boundless. He wants to elevate us . . . take us to a place where we can soar (a place more expansive than we can see or have envisioned). He wants to take us to that place where "eye hath not seen, nor ear heard...that place that he hath prepared for us because we love him." It's a place of TRUST. (*1 Cor. 2:9*)

I need to take a little time to let this rest.

Chapter 4

Resuscitation

Psalm 23:3 (KJV) "He restoreth my soul: he leadeth me in the paths of righteousness for his name's sake."

Resuscitate – revive; make active or vigorous again

After God leads us beside the "still waters" and makes certain that we are "still in agreement," he restores us. In other words, He resuscitates us. When I began working on this chapter in April of 2020, I began to ponder what awakens the baby (gift). Initially, I did a little research on resurrection because I was thinking in the line of raising from the dead, but when I looked it up, it meant bringing something/someone back to life that is literally dead. However, as I was looking at being Still Born, I couldn't get settled in that. I then heard the word resuscitation. So, I began to look at the difference between the two. To resuscitate, on the other hand, means "to revive from unconsciousness or apparent death." (*oxfordlanguage.com*) Apparent just indicates that something appears to be a certain way. I kept going back and forth until God settled in my spirit that we are looking at resuscitation.

Now, here I am in August 2022, after this work has had some time to rest, that God is opening my eyes even more clearly as to what this means. When it comes to resuscitating, let's look at the word unconscious. It says that it is the part of the mind that is "inaccessible to the conscious mind but still affects behavior and emotions." (*oxfordlanguagedic-*

tionary) You know how you hear people say or we even say sometimes, "I know what God has given me to do or I believe I'm supposed to be doing a certain thing, but it's dead or useless. There's no way I'll be able to do it. It's too late." When we look back at the gift, God will not allow our conscious mind to access it, but He does allow it to affect our emotions. The desire is still there; it's just the belief system that has been compromised. The vision is still there. God has it on life support. We just don't have access to it until it has been resuscitated. In other words, we are not in control of it. God decides when we can fully access it.

This is a good place to take a rest break.

I need to take a moment to reflect on my notes from March 28, 2021. At that point, God began to deal with me about the state of the gift. In that comatose state, He's working on the mind or the soul, aligning it with His spirit (if we allow Him). We could step into it prematurely, but we won't have full access to the gift. In this instance, people are operating with an un-resuscitated gift. The gift is not dead; it's just not fully accessible. Just as in the natural, a person is not dead as long as their brain is alive. Consequently, the bodily functions are inactive as long as life support is necessary.

An interesting fact is that the heart never pauses to rest. In most instances, we won't stop and rest on our own so God has to help us. He temporarily puts us (our gift, our calling/our assignment/our baby) in a state of rest. He has it under cardiac arrest . . . temporarily locked up. WHEN HE ARRESTS US, He disconnects the heart (activity/movement) from the brain (the mind, will, and emotions) for the period of time He needs to prepare us. The gift still lives because its brain is still alive. He took me to *Jeremiah 17:9-10* which states,

9 "The heart is deceitful above all things, and desperately wicked: who can know it? **10** I the Lord search the heart, I try the reins, even to give every man according to his ways, and according to the fruit of his doings."

According to *Strong's Concordance*, the heart (the feelings, the will, the intellect) is deceitful (fraudulent, crooked, polluted) and desperately wicked (frail, melancholy, sick). So, God has to search us (examine us intimately). He does it while we are still because we are not going to hear Him clearly while we are constantly moving, running all over the place, trying to make things happen.

While He has us on trial, He examines the "reins" (mind) and appoints/assigns based on our mode of action or course of life and works. As I was analyzing this verse, this thought came to mind. Naturally speaking, it takes the brain and the heart functioning properly to live. Spiritually speaking, the gift cannot manifest unless the brain and the heart are working together. The heart needs to be right if the gift is going to become mobile for His glory. He took me to John **15:2-5** (KJV).

> **2** "Every branch in me that beareth not fruit he taketh away: and every branch that beareth fruit, he purgeth it, that it may bring forth more fruit. **3** Now ye are clean through the word which I have spoken unto you. **4** Abide in me, and I in you. As the branch cannot bear fruit of itself, except it abide in the vine; no more can ye, except ye abide in me. **5** I am the vine, ye are the branches: He that abideth in me, and I in him, the same bringeth forth much fruit: for without me ye can do nothing."

Remember, during this comatose state, we are "still" (inactive, unable to move). When God gets through pruning us (working on our hearts and getting rid of the useless, unnecessary, and undesirable stuff we don't need or whatever is hindering our spiritual growth), he begins to repeatedly press on that gift. When we are ready to go forth, He gives us CPR (Cardiopulmonary Resuscitation). He restores blood circulation and brings the gift back to life. He continues to breathe new life (His purpose/His mission/His plan/His power/His anointing) so that we are able to go forth in Him... with His seal of approval.

This takes us back to *Psalms 23:3b*. After he restoreth our souls, *"He leadeth us in the paths of righteousness for his name's sake."*

HE RESTORES LIFE, VITALITY, and ACTIVITY because now we are ready to follow Him.

Chapter 5

Take Up Thy Bed And Walk

John 5:2 "Now there is at Jerusalem by the sheep market a pool, which is called in the Hebrew tongue Bethesda, having five porches."

5:5 "And a certain man was there, which had an infirmity thirty and eight years."

5:6 "When Jesus saw him lie, and knew that he had been now a long time in that case, he saith unto him, Wilt thou be made whole?"

5:7 "The impotent man answered him, Sir, I have no man, when the water is troubled, to put me into the pool: but while I am coming, another steppeth down before me."

5:8 "Jesus saith unto him, Rise, take up thy bed, and walk."

5:9 "And immediately the man was made whole, and took up his bed, and walked: and on the same day was the sabbath."

Walk – to follow a certain course of life or to conduct oneself in a certain way; to live.

I found it quite interesting that God began to breathe this chapter into my spirit on October 24, 2020 as I was casually observing the neighborhood during my daily 3 mile-walk which had turned into a time of deep meditation. At that time, He was dealing with me about taking up my bed and walking from a figurative perspective. Now, here I am two years later, beginning to revise/edit the final draft of this chapter while experiencing some physical challenges with walking.

I had finally made up my mind to begin moving and get this finished, and this distraction arises. I'm striving to move forward, but my mobility had been compromised. My first thought was to just set everything aside and prayerfully come back to it later when I was feeling better, but God would not allow me to even become comfortable with that thought. What better time to write about walking than this, a time within the press... putting pressure on the pressure. I can understand what Paul meant in *Philippians 3:13-14* about pressing "toward the mark." I've got to "reach forth." The pursuit is on!

So, let's travel back to October 2020. I'm struggling in the midst of the Pandemic, trying to figure out what I'm going to do and how I'm going to move forward. I'm in a state of paralysis. I can remember a lot of walking, a lot of praying, and a lot of crying. I know what the Lord had shown me for so many years, but things looked really dim. The Lord began to deal with me about the man at the pool of Bethesda in *John Chapter 5*. There was a man who had been suffering from an infirmity for 38 years. In verse 6 Jesus asked him, "Wilt thou be made whole?" Although he tried to rationalize as to why he hadn't been made whole in all of those years, he made a decision that day to trust Jesus. Because of that, he was immediately made whole.

Oftentimes we look at our situations and circumstances, especially when it's something that we've been dealing with for many many years. Every time we try to move but face opposition, we guard ourselves by putting up walls because of the fear of failure. We start second-guessing our ability to do what we've been called to do. God has already put in us everything that we need, but we allow the Enemy to trick or trap us in a maze of fear.

The Lord led me back to verse 5 in *John* Chapter 5 to look at the period of time the man had had an infirmity. At the time I was walking, I wasn't looking at the reference, but I could remember that there was an eight in the number. I continued to meditate, and I kept hearing 18 years in my spirit, but I knew that the man's infirmity was a lot longer than eighteen. So, when I went back and looked at the verse, it was 38 years.

At that point, I was trying to figure out, "So, why 18, because the scripture said 38?" I was trying to see the connection, but God confirmed that I needed to focus on 18. (That was for me). I knew there was a connection between what happened with the man at the Pool and something He was trying to show me in my own life, but I was trying to over-spiritualize the numbers. He was downloading so many things as I was finishing my walk. By the time I made it home, things began to unfold. He took me down a numerical journey to help me see how He moves and how He works over time. He said, "The man's infirmity (weakness) was **38** years but yours is **18** years." The man couldn't move, and I couldn't move. God was establishing a pattern for me at that time. **HE BEGAN TO WALK ME THROUGH THE TIMELINE.**

But, I'm still thinking, "***Why 18?***"

As I began to continually deal with this chapter, I began to see more clearly as to the significance of the number 18 in my life. Numerically, 18 is made up of the numbers one and eight which represent new beginnings and abundance. Prophetically speaking, 18 means "alive." I can see how this connects to what God unfolded. Just like the man at the pool, my obedience to His voice awakened something on the inside of me. Remember, I'm actually writing this in **2020**, but God took me back to **2002**. He gave me several assignments in **2002** (which was **18** years ago) that I began working on, but because they didn't fully manifest, I gave up on the work. God began to show me several other significant facts about 18 that stood out. I accepted my calling in **May 1989** but was not licensed until **March 25, 2007** – [18 years later]. Also, in the Summer of **2018**, I started a Youth Ministry for teens from our church, but it only lasted for a short period of time.

God has spent several years preparing me for this journey. I was trying to fulfill my assignments, but I just wasn't paying attention to the timing (or the season). Actually, in my immaturity, I didn't really think it mattered when...just as long as I was trying. And, because I wasn't making the connection, I was always frustrated when things didn't work out as I had planned.

In 2015, God allowed me to retire from teaching in the public school system to begin ministry full-time. But, at that time, I thought he was calling me out solely so that I could spend more time in music as a career. So, I tirelessly put so much time and effort into that pursuit that the ministry work that was more significant to God came up lacking. I did the work, but my heart leaned toward the music, and I became consumed with it. I allowed some fears and challenges to deter me, and I continued with what I was more comfortable with, The Path of Least Resistance. In all that I did, things did not work out the way that I had anticipated they would.

God began to show me some other significant things that happened in the year 2018 that were very impactful in my life. I had become discouraged and wanted to give up on what God had promised. Our Church had a special service for me on April 22, 2018. It was a TOTAL surprise. It ignited something in me. The message was "Go Deeper."

Now, as I am writing, I can see how that message directly connects to this 2020 experience with taking up my bed and walking, stepping into the water. . . but going deeper. I didn't understand it then, but I understand it now. Also, around that same time in 2018, I began planning our 2020 Women's Redemption Retreat. I had no clue at that time that in 2020, there would be a COVID-19 shut down and that I was going to be the only one at the retreat.

God allowed me to plan it out elaborately. Then He orchestrated things so that He and I would be the only ones in attendance. It was a one-day retreat scheduled for June 20, 2020 which turned into a 5-month journey. But, God is so gracious, and it's quite interesting how He works.

I found it so interesting how prophetic this was because 2020 was a LEAP Year. While I was reviewing this, I began to notice that the timing is actually right in line with God's timing because from 2002 to 2020 was the 18th year – the year of a powerful shift and move of God in my life.

I was instantly taken back to my first music project entitled "God Wants to Speak To You." He took me to a place that enabled me to write music that would make a difference in the lives of people. I'm like, "Oh, my God, what are you saying in the midst of all of this?" He wanted me to take the initiative, stop waiting on someone else to do certain things for me, or stop stressing when others moved ahead before me. In **verse 7**, Jesus asked the man *"Wilt thou be made whole?"* In other words, do you want it? If you want to be healed, you've got to do something. When Jesus spoke in verse 9, the man was made whole immediately; he just believed, got up, and got moving. His faith and obedience made him whole. That's what God was saying to me. "Just be obedient. I am with you."

The next thing He showed me was awesome. When He sent me out in 2002 to begin the assignment, I took another path. Now, 18 years later, (2020), He's releasing me to go forth again, but with grace (making my way easier). But, look at the years: 2002 and 2020. They consist of the same numbers. If you move the last 2 in 2002 to the left, it becomes 20. The numbers are the same. Whether this manifested in 2002 or 2020, it STILL happened.

Chapter 6

Weight... On the Lord

Hebrews 12:1 (KJV)

"Wherefore seeing we also are compassed about with so great a cloud of witnesses, let us lay aside every weight, and the sin which doth so easily beset us, and let us run with patience the race that is set before us."

Weight – a mass or load that is a burden (hindrance)

This chapter's title stemmed from a conversation my daughter and I were having on December 14, 2021, about goals, how to proceed forward, and plans for the future. Her thoughts were "on the run." She was looking at my being retired and able to move at my own pace in life. She said "See I'm trying to get like you. I want to be retired by age 35, and I want to do this and that and so on and so forth." This sparked another conversation about pacing.

The next morning when I got up, I heard this thought rise up in my spirit, "Wait on the Lord. If you Wait... He'll take the Weight." Suddenly, everything started coming together. I kept hearing, "Let us lay aside every weight, and the sin which doth so easily beset us, and let us run with patience the race that is set before us." (*Hebrews 12:1*) Then I began to hear Psalm 27:14 which encourages us to *"Wait on the LORD: be of good courage, and he shall strengthen thine heart: wait, I say, on the LORD."* The Holy Spirit also brought back to my remembrance *Isaiah 40:31* which states, "But they that wait upon the Lord shall renew their strength; they shall mount up with wings as eagles; they shall run, and not be weary; and they shall walk, and not faint." I then heard the Lord say, "Your inability or reluctance to W.A.I.T became a W-E-I-G-H-T."

As I have been waiting to finish this chapter without the weight (pressure) of finishing it in the time I had originally set, God has brought it all together. I'm finding out more and more how waiting requires patience. I love what *James 1:4* (NKJV) says. "But let patience have its perfect work, that you may be perfect [mature] and complete, lacking nothing." Patience enables us to pace ourselves for endurance. Spiritually speaking, God tries to slow us down before we become overloaded; however, when we refuse to pace ourselves, He has to help us. He slows things down to where they should be so that we can settle down. Then we will be able to continue the race.

As I was continually taken back to Hebrews 12:1, Part b illuminated. It says, *"Let us run with patience the race THAT IS SET BEFORE US."* This confirms that the race is already set (fixed) even before we get started." Because it has been predetermined, there is nothing we can do to change it. So the Big Question is, "What are we pressing (striving) toward?" *Philippians 3:14* teaches that we should "press toward the mark for the prize of the high calling of God in Christ Jesus." In other words, we should be pursuing Jesus, and if we pursue Him, God will take care of the rest. Lay aside the weight, and wait on Him because "Jesus is the author and finisher of our faith." *Hebrews 12:2* (KJV)

Whatever God has assigned is still going to be done...but at His pace. I can think of several instances in my life where my faith was tested because of my inability to wait. God paces us to keep it ALL ABOUT HIM!!! See, our steps are "ordered by God." When we ask God to order our steps, we're actually saying, "Pace me, O God." I have learned that what it means to take steps not only means moving forward but it also means making the necessary preparations before we begin. Psalm 119:133 says, *"Order my steps in thy word: and let not any iniquity have dominion over me."* In other words, we are asking God to prepare us or get us ready before we begin moving. Prepare us through your word. Help us make proper provisions. Give us the directions and instructions on what you want us to do and how you want us to do it. As I was writing this, I heard Him say, "IF YOU 'WAIT' ON ME, THE 'WEIGHT' IS ON ME."

When God gave the title, I wasn't sure how everything would unfold, but as I continued to meditate and write, He began to show me the prophetic side of "weight" in this chapter. If you remove the "W" from the word "weight," you have the word "eight." God had actually been setting me up to see the Significant Power of the number Eight in my life, which means new beginnings. He showed me the importance of 18 in the previous chapter before He led me to the number 8. At that point He instantly began to walk me down memory lane.

The Power of Eight

There were several instances, but these are the ones that stood out most.

- I was born on the 8th day of the month.

- I began playing for 3 of my Dad's churches at 8 years old.

- I wrote my first original song during the Ice Storm of 1994 entitled "You Can Make It Through The Storm," which was written 8 years after I began my teaching career.

- In 2002, I graduated from Exodus School of the Bible and completed my first Life Experience Portfolio in Ministry, which was 8 years after I wrote my first original song.

- I started writing several books in 2002. Only one was completed 8 years later.

- I was married in the 8th month of the year.

- I was licensed to preach 8 years before I retired.

- Although I retired to go into ministry full time; notably, it manifested 8 years later.

After I had my 58th birthday, God spoke a word in my spirit that I have been graced for new beginnings. So, now I will purposely embrace the newness that He constantly brings. I will be more attentive to things that connect to 8 in my life so that I can see how He desires to move and how He desires me to move.

God chooses how He is going to move in each of our lives. That is why we have to seek Him for ourselves and allow Him to show us His pattern, His plan, His timing, and His season for us individually. Remember, He is not late. He is just handling the weight as we wait on our "due" date. *Galatians 6:9 [KJV]*

Chapter 7

Worth the Wait

As I was thinking about everything that I have been believing God for and how things are beginning to manifest, I can truly see now how it has all been worth the wait. I can see more clearly how the different phases of "still" have impacted and will continue to impact my life and my development for the advancement of the Kingdom. Stillness is drawing me even closer to God than I have ever been and now I know "with certainty, assurance, and understanding" that He is who He says He is and He stands on His promises. I realize that everything is inevitably in His hands. I just have to wait patiently for it. He didn't take back what He birthed in me, and He hasn't taken back what He has birthed in you. It's still there.

Even from the beginning of time, according to **Genesis 1**, God saw "everything that he had made, and, behold, [it was] very good." As I was writing this, I noticed that He used the verb "***was***," which is the past tense of the verb "***is***." Therefore, whatever He speaks into our lives is created and approved at the same time. Immediately, after He speaks, the process becomes past tense for us. We have to stand on what He said (spoke). When He says it, it is settled.

Our challenge becomes the PROCESS... Walking out in the present what was already completed in the past. In other words, walking out what God has shown us through the steps that have been ordered by Him. The *Revised Standard Version (RSV)* of **Psalm 119:133** says, "Keep steady my steps *according to thy promise,* and let no iniquity (wickedness/idols) get dominion (power) over me." **According to Jeremiah 29:11** (KJV), God has good thoughts about us, "thoughts of peace, and not of evil, to give an expected end." Therefore, we need to step into the stillness. It's just God's way of protecting what we have been expecting.

Embrace the challenges and struggles and disappointments and setbacks and things that appear to be roadblocks or hindrances. Just allow yourself to settle down and dig deeper and deeper into your spirit to truly see what God desires of you FOR HIS PURPOSE . . . FOR HIS GLORY. The gift is still there. God birthed it in your spirit, but it's up to Him when it will fully manifest. The simple fact that you are alive and breathing indicates or signifies that God is giving you another opportunity to prepare for the fulfillment of His will for your life. Don't give up! Don't quit! Just get up, dust yourself off, wipe your tears, and get prepared to do it.

So, from now on, if someone asks when something is going to happen or manifest in your life, your response should be "**STILL**."

Still . . . Believing

Still . . . Trusting

Still . . . Waiting

In other words, you are walking in the confidence that because God spoke it, He is going to do what He said He would do when He is ready to do it at the level that He desires it to be done. *Ecclesiastes 3:1* confirms, "*To everything, there is a season, and a time to every purpose under the heaven.*" In conjunction, Galatians 6:9 states that we should "*not be weary in well doing: for in due season we shall reap, if we faint not.*" Keep *Numbers 23:19* close to your heart. "God is not a man, that he should lie; neither the son of man, that he should repent." If He said it, HE is **STILL** going to do it? Or if **HE** spoke it, **HE** is **STILL** going to make it good.

My Daily Prayer
Glenda Woods

Lord, I surrender my all to you.
Thank you for forgiving me of all my sins
And cleansing me from all unrighteousness.
Lead and guide me in my pursuit of holiness.
Walk with me as I shake off worldly conformation
And embrace spiritual transformation.
Renew my mind through your word.
As you renew my mind, create in me a clean heart
And renew a right spirit within me.
Show yourself strong in every aspect of my life

Because my greatest desire is to
please you
As I am being conformed into the image
of your Son.
Not my will, oh God,
But let thine will be done in my life in
Jesus' name.

References

Biblical

Unless otherwise indicated, all scripture quotations are taken from the King James Version of the Holy Bible.

The author cites from various noted Biblical translations, including:

- King James Version [KJV]
- Blue Letter Bible [BLB]
- New Living Translation [NLT]
- New English Translation [NET]
- Revised Standard Version [RSV]
- KJV Study Bible
- Strong's Bible Concordance
- kingjamesbibleonline.org
- kingjamesbibledictionary.com
- biblestudytools.com

Additional

- wikipedia.org

References

- investopedia.com
- oxfordlanguagedictionary.com
- merriam-webster.com

Numbers 23:19

God is not a man, that he should lie;
Neither the son of man, that he should repent:
Hath he said, and shall he not do it?
Or hath he spoken, and shall he not make it good?

www.ingramcontent.com/pod-product-compliance
Lightning Source LLC
Chambersburg PA
CBHW062004180426
43198CB00036B/2350